Adam Wonders

An unauthorized collection from the heart and
mind of Adam Elliott Davis

January 1–August 31, 2015

Adam Elliott Davis

Edited by Marty Beaudet

Published in the United States by Dinkus Books.

ISBN: 978-0-9893580-0-2

All photos by Adam Elliott Davis,
except where noted.

Dinkus Books
13825 SE 180th Avenue
Damascus, Oregon 97089-8280
www.funbookstoread.com

For Adam, whose friendship
I will always treasure.

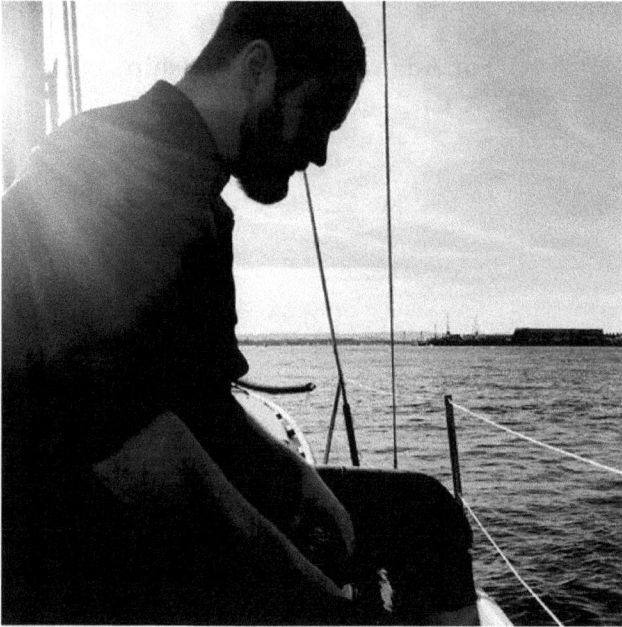

Photo: Tricia Marie Castañeda-Gonzales

Ode to all the positivity clogging up Facebook:

I new year's kissed the future,
Whose lips were made for me.
I held her close as I would dare
And heard her melody.

We danced until the morning,
And in her eyes were stars,
And every sweet tomorrow
Was tangled in her arms.

My tongue was tied with whiskey
But she still spoke my name
And told me how she'd love to see
Our destinations same.

And there upon horizons,
On mornings where she lives,
We'll meet in sweet forevers
With mysteries she gives.

For I new year's kissed the heavens,
And took her hand in mine,
And promised her my passion,
And she promised me her time.

January 1, 2015

Communication is a gift: to speak and be heard; to write and be read; to give lines, and receive them with no need for whatever is between. Between the lines rest mysteries and conspiracies, pain, confusion, endless struggles between heart and head, and sometimes even beauty and love and magic. But on the page, in the ink, there is simply poetry, simply the heartbeat, simply the truth, and sometimes, that's enough.

January 5, 2015

Joy, T.M.

Talk for hours, joy
Your eyes are blue then green
There's proof of something true in them
There's something there, unseen.
Talk for days, then none
I hear all your heart beats
I swear there's something blue in them
There's something there for me.
Talk of weeks of winter
Pray alone for snow
Tell me all your moments, dear
There's something in your glow.
Take these months in measure
The new year's just begun
You work harder than everybody
You're harder than anyone.

And in your eyes a memory,
And in your smile a kiss,
And in your hands the ring
Falling from your fingertips

It's cold outside for longing
Too cold outside to stay
But stay one moment longer,
So we may talk for days.

For even with these broken pictures,
fixtures fitting memories in seas of ancient
broken hearts and bloody wrists and
wounded knees, and brothers- fallen
soldiers brave and famous feelings fleeting
fade, find me there beside you lover, in the
summer, in the day; we say we're fighting
separate seasons, treasons deep in seas
unfold, but even these will be made even
when our skies have turned to gold, so
hold on lover, others may not see the
victories in store, but keep your fire, oh
my summer, faster than you have before,
adore you, I do, face for pictures,
scriptures read and stitches spread and
stretched across old cuts and bruises,
sutures used for lovely uses, token broken
hearts in pieces, these we'll tie with scarlet
thread, and hand-in-hand if dear you'll
have me, laugh we run as fast we fled, we
chase those dreams and capture all the
promises we ever plead. Beauty, grace,
gazelle, make haste to chase the sun to its
horizon, find it hiding there beside the Joy
you keep inside and bind it then to mine, I
promise you, I'm strong enough to carry

all the burdens that I bear and bury them beneath the golden shores. The course is clear to me my dear, and hear me if you may and stay and say you'll see what days may bring, you Joy, blue eyes, then green, with me.

January 6, 2015

New sun kissing bare skin on a warm day- the tactile equal to the sound of a twinkling laugh. A good laugh from a beautiful face is a crashing wave- a smile and big eyes, the diamonds that paint the sea. Lovely words from lovelier lips, cotton clouds swimming across the sky. Yesterday was summer, and I was basking in it.

January 7, 2015

She's pure and perfect velvet.
Her flaws, she has none, though she sees
them as such; to me, they are stars. Every
freckle, every scar, they are constellations:
this one the lover, that one the warrior,
that one even, the queen. The mole on her
skin is a jewel- a treasure uncovered only
by a careful hand; even she doesn't know
it's there. The silver in her hair is filament,
her precious woven crown, her wisdom,
even in her youth; glory.
Her eyes hold shadows; they are mysteries,
legends, beautiful stories of strength and
victories I long to hear with a hunger. And
there, in her perfect orbs, a light flashes
lively and sure; and in that light, vibrant
futures, a thousand more perfect victories,
a solemn promise against surrender- the
truth of her tenacity- for in her eyes
casting shadows is a flame burning
brighter with every smile.
And she is warm to the touch.
And she is pure and perfect velvet.

January 11, 2015

The Day We Lost Our Words

Fumbling through the dark, we looked for
skin, we looked for bones,
We found each other, found tomorrow,
found forever, home.
Left for morning where we left it, where
we woke up, with the snow
With the tempest, with the rain clouds,
with the winter, with the glow.
We promised nothing, nothing needed,
nothing spoken, something heard
On that gold and silver morning when at
last we lost our words
There within the pillows, there in
blankets, there we were
To quietly discover everything we found
without our words.
And soft outside her window, only birds
into their song did break,
As softly on her pillow to my mouth her

crimson lips did take

And silently forever in that moment just
our love would make

Our words so swiftly disappear there in
that moment where we wake.

Just up to the sunrise, just in quiet, just in
peace, justice

Take my mourning melancholy heart into
your hands' release

For the time is fast and growing old, my
dear, we'll ever be

And in storms, in hurricanes, in summer
rain, in love you'll see

That though we shake and run and faint
and fall and break and bleed,

My hands are tough with toil and arms are
strong to carry thee,

And to the mountain, to the summit, to
the stars we'll climb,

And you can take my shaky hands and I

can take your time.

Up there in skies too blue for sorrow,

much too true for care,

We'll chase the galaxies we claim and take

them if we dare.

For thereupon the mountain top my dear

we will be heard:

The heroes found the future on the day

they lost their words.

January 13, 2015

At any given moment, I wish I were
better. I wish I was stronger, leaner, more
capable.

I wish my voice was clearer when it's not,
and my words were better suited.

It's safe to say that in this moment, I wish
I were kinder, softer, braver, more
practical.

I wish my vices would disappear, and leave
me with simpler love, deeper rooted.

If only every song I wrote could be a
symphony, and every note painted red
with meaning,

And every line I traced down pages perfect
in its form, for each its own end suited,

And every simple statement, every "thank
you," every "I love you" its own reward
repeating.

How fine it would seem, if everything I
tried with my might would gain the reward

I had planned,

But my might isn't quite as mighty as even

I wish it would be, not as valiant an effort,

And even when I "do my best," the "best" I

do falls somewhat short of the "best" I

demand.

After all, even my most prolific, by

comparison, is simply a drop of rain in a

desert.

If all my words landed upon listening ears,

perhaps I could be complete.

And if every touch I shared was electric,

then my skin would not so crave.

If my eyes looked once upon the prize and

never away, I'd more fully see,

And every kiss was every kiss, then lips

would be the sunlight upon every crashing

wave.

If I simply could have said, could have

done, could then be,

Maybe then I'd not so need, not so want,
not so search,
Maybe then I'd finally have, finally know,
finally see,
And every song I sang would be the music
just her heart had heard.

But then, I'd be a stone.
I'd be a solemn tree.
I'd learn no more, and love no less,
And stand passionlessly.
I'd never taste the need to work,
I'd never hope to grow,
I'd never find the fight within,
And never seeds I'd sow.

So maybe it's okay then,
I'm not quite yet what I wish,
And perhaps the morning air I breathe in
Will be brand new and crisp.
I'll fill my lungs with victories,

I'd otherwise not see,

For the best of reaching what I wish

Is starting first at me.

And tonight, I'll want for nothing. I'll work for the mountain top, and pray for the grace to know just what to say.

January 15, 2015

Love like rails, heartbeat, sunset,

Words like sails, you're my horizon.

Skin like whispers, softly, smooth, let

All your breaths escape, collide in

This sweet, silent, motionless now.

This tender bliss, quiet, comfort.

Make your move dear, darling, slow how

You can do so perfect, tender.

This great distance- closes, opens

Unto morning, lover, linger

For the day may take us, over

But I feel your smile, fingers,

Lips and lashes, flutter, taste you

Stay forever, farther, nearer

Close your eyes and let me chase you.

From greater distance, hearts are clearer.

January 19, 2015

January 27, 2015

Imagine, if you will, an ocean, a bay.
Upon it, golden shores of lonely isles; the
horizon, hidden in the distance. Sunrise.
Tuesday.

I miss her skin,

Those starlit speckled rolling lines,

The velvet on her gentle curves

The lightning from her moonlit eyes.

The fiction in her crossing arms

And friction from her fingertips,

The way her words are caged behind

The loveliness of crimson lips.

The way her chin so pointedly

Will point itself away from me,

Her feet too sore from standing

All the hours in the day she sees,

And how her legs

Are pedestals

That flow like language

Up her bones,

Up to her ribs

Where therein lies

The gentle heart

Beating inside,

Where coyly there it hammers phrases
Delicate, into the wind
That whispers through the world like
mazes
Finishing at last on skin;
And there complete the supple grace
Of youth and beauty on her face
Does finally yet know its place
To sweetly rest upon her skin.

February 6, 2015

With flowers in her hair,
I swear I saw her standing there
A thousand miles in her stare
Searching for a dream to care.
And in the summer where she stood
All the light on her was good
All the music on her lips
Were all the songs I never could-
For she was rivers, she was snow
She was moonlight, she was glow
She was oceans in the morning,
She was beauty just to know
That her hands would soon be held
And her sky would fill with bells
And that there her heart would swell
She was poetry to tell
With that sunlight in her eyes
And the pearls in her smile
And the diamonds in her skies
She was always worth the while
When I found her standing there
All her futures in her stare
All her lovely songs to share
All those blossoms in her hair.

February 6, 2015

She chooses every letter carefully;

Every syllable perfectly curated on her lips,

She speaks in the spaces between sounds,

And I hang on every. Single. Silence.

Her voice is like a phonograph record,

Where even the dust is filled with beauty,

For every note she crafts behind her teeth

Is the truest definition of music.

February 13, 2015

Sometimes, beauty is described in
thousands of words. Sometimes, it is
described best in a handful of letters.
Sometimes, a name.

February 17, 2015

Sometimes still I like to dream,
A thousand miles anonymously,
That stretched there out under my feet
And found me standing at your door.

And in my hand, a promise kept
The land unlooked for, only leapt,
Where up into the sky were swept
Those words we share, I love you more.

Then from that near-perfect bliss,
You collapse into my kiss,
So still I taste you on my lips
And find you where you were before.

Run through cathedrals, chasing trains
Finding summer, dance the rains
All your music's sweet refrains
Echoing still through my core.

For there we were like memory,
And there we'll go like melody,
A thousand miles anonymously,
Until I'm standing at your door.

February 22, 2015

To the pretty girl at the center of the room that one time:

For fear now of spilling my words on the
floor, I implore you dear vision this river
ignore, for its current is carried out now
from my lips not by might nor by will but
by gravity, this
Is quite simply a force as by nature
conveyed, and far and beyond my
attempts to contain
And restrain myself, yes, all the terms you
command, and every one a deserving
demand
But here I am lady, just staring, it seems,
right into the sun now for all that it
means,
When your image is burned to the back of
my eyes, from your legs to your lips, to
your clouds, to your skies,
To your eyes back to mine, to your heart,

to your mind, to your words so impossible, perfect, refined,
To the way you inspire such whimsical rhymes, and even your smile perfectly defined.

So darling, allow me to tell you this secret,
A rule, if you will, for the way this will go,
Patiently waiting will be my demeanor,
And patiently waiting is how you will know,
That I will want nothing more than your sweet smile,
And I will give nothing more than my whole heart
For I have nothing to offer except, dear,
The finest, most perfect, most valuable art:
That being the kiss when you'll tell me you love me

That being the smile you press to my face,

That being the song in my heart when I

see you,

And knowing the music is filling the place

In my chest where your language will live

like the summer

And blossom like spring with its million

blooms,

And your kindness is healing a lifetime of

breaking

And building like houses with millions of

rooms,

And painting old bruises with porcelain

and pure;

And stitching together old breaks in old

bones,

And replacing skipped heartbeats with

simple and quiet

And sunlight, and held hands, and coming

back home.

And there, my darling,

Like the morning sun rises,

You will be golden.

As you are now, burned into the back of
my eyes.

March 9, 2015

Sometimes when I see you, my brain can't comprehend it. My mind grows quiet, and simply takes you in. When I want to elaborate, I can only think in ideas, never complete sentences. Porcelain, beauty, sharpness, and song. You are the colors and the lines.

The soft things and the fragile things, you are among them. The delicate and the rare, they are common by comparison. A photograph couldn't capture your glow, nor a still-frame your verve. Here is me, in awe of all that's conspired to make you. Your father must be proud, and your mother must be overjoyed. You are the thousand words.

(and now that you know...)

March 13, 2015

I met you in a dream,

A thousand years ago it seems,

And sweetly there our words did play,

So perfectly into the day

Where all our lives did safely dwell

The miracle, the solemn bell,

The whispered wand'rings of your speech,

The gentle velvet of your cheek.

Your lips were redder than the sun

Where it kisses the horizon.

You were dancing, twirling lovely

Next to me, above me,

In the night, into the dream

Where I met you and it did seem

As though your beauty'd be forever,

And our hands would tie together,

But we'd age into the sunset,

And grow old until we forget

That I met you in a dream,

And you were dancing there with me,

And the night I saw your face,

And heard your voice my heartstrings
trace,

I knew I'd finally managed

The right time, and the right place.

I met you in a dream, and you were
dancing.

I haven't woken up yet. I hope I never
will.

March 28, 2015

You are my star. My hero, my friend. The brightest light in the night sky, you are a pin-hole into the wonders of the day. I may not always see you. You may not always be mine to find. But I know you're up there waiting, watching for my life to shine. You are the north, even when there's no north to see, and the way home truly, for I may ever follow thee. You are my hero in a heroless land of simple soldiers, and a Father when no father do I find. My heart is large and beats as a thousand drums just to come but closer to your wonderful design. I'm nothing much, but something, not for any effort I've maintained. Rather, I'm a vehicle for your prefect plans in me sustained. I only hope I may offer some of the light in me you gave- to everyone around me so they only see your smiling face. For, I know I am darkness. The shadow of my life is deep. But I will wake in prefect sun, vibrant where my soul you keep. I falter with each day that rises, sets, then breaks again. I'm weak and feeble, crass and evil, knowing not what fate I tend, but still you love me, even against those who hate my simple soul, and here you are, even when I fall, waiting to make me whole. So thank you for your grace, and thank you for every moment you give, to love, to live, to grieve, to create, to grow, to build, to touch, to give- I am nothing without you, and nothing shall I ever be, would it not for you to make my blind and desperate heart to see. My love, my hero, my safe and perfect calm, I wish I could convey to every single heart how great you are- how you live with open arms and do not war or fight or strive, but give endlessly to us because you gave endlessly your life.

April 1, 2015

Her voice is a light in the dark,
A breeze in the mist,
As she sails there across the sea.

At night she beckons,
Like moonlight dancing slow,
Over waters next to me.

I run my fingers through,
Her weightless heav'nly glow,
And feel her words so gentle in my soul.

And there I'll keep the song,
Safely burned into the phonograph,
As then upon my lonely way I go.

So I may ever play,
Within the horn of my heart,
Every lovely song she ever wrote.

And sing it back to her,
Softly then in the stillness,
With every single heartbeat that she stole.

April 1, 2015

The Island of the Sea

There lives out there,
And just above,
The Island of the Sea.

It floats upon
The waves just so,
Aglow in sun and green.

Upon its shores
Are golden sands,
Where ships have found their rest.

And just beyond,
In verdant sway,
Are forests richly blessed.

Rising high
Above the trees,
A mountain touches sky,

And stars alight
An evening veil
To kiss the sea goodbye.

T'was upon
This mountain top
I made my sweet repose.

I built a home,
In which alone,
I'd give my eyes to close.

For once upon a time,
I landed
On that lovely beach,

In search of that
Which I had heard
Was ever out of reach.

And there I looked,
Through wood and stone,
For treasures yet unknown,

For all I'd heard
Were legends of this
Glory to be shown.

But there I stayed,
In desperate quest
This mysterious gift,

And found at times
What'd only be
Mirage my spirits lift.

T'was upon
This island lost
I thought I'd surely die,

For no hope
Was I to find
That there my treasure lie.

At last I climbed
That mountain tall
To rest at Heaven's gate,

And while away
The days and nights
In melancholy wait.

But suddenly
One sunset sweet
Did something find my eye!

There ashore,
Another ship
Had landed on my isle.

I left my home
Of solitude,
And stumbled to the sea.

So alone I'd been
My love,
I'd never stopped to be

Patiently
Awaiting waves
To bring that gift to me.

And when I saw you,
On the sand,
The gravity let free.

For something you
Did long pursue
But didn't know the name,

Was the treasure
I did know,
This gift, the very same.

And when it seems
We ended then
Our looking at long last,

That the sea
Did call our names,
And gather us but fast.

So, beloved,
Magically, you mystery
My glee,

Stay with me,
In love, upon
Our Island of the Sea.

April 1, 2015

"**Thank you for being kind**," she said,

As though I was doing a favor,

And there into the night she went

With me as just her neighbor,

But what she doesn't understand

Is that she's all of beauty,

And every way I could respond

Was only to my duty.

And as she walked into her room

With that new beau in waiting,

I could then only see her face

And think of her there saying

That "maybe once there would be love

Or perhaps something better

But now you are the boy for whom

I couldn't dream of whether

You might or not be everything

My dear, I'd ever hope for,"

And there my darling then I left you

Just beyond your door, for

You're so much a masterpiece,

I'd never right explain it,

So as you walk away with him

I know my heart will paint it.

For all the colors that you are,

And every single lesson

Is everything I need to learn,

And there I'll find my blessing.

My dear
There you are,
So near,
And so far.
So I wait
For you
To come home.

April 6, 2015

This isn't a smile-

It's a scar I cut across my face to make space in an attempt to display grace and show this human race the face that was saved in disgrace, replacing the twisted wounds and old bruises- these crocodile tears I abuse are useless amusements that give sneak peaks at the abuses I'm used to, from way back when I used to give myself wholly to every single one and only, then trampled, stampeded, rampaged, beaten senseless and bleeding from putting this heart out there one too many times, trusting in once upon a time's and time and again the friend I believed in took all that I designed to receive, then threw it back at me rusty, broken, corrupted and dusty. Mistreated, so many times I seem to be misleading, it's a chronic defeating, it's a bitter old lonely I can't get over, it

holds me and broke me, became less of a
stronghold and more of a home, see after a
while I forgot how to be myself, after too
many knife wounds you put your guts on a
shelf and live in a shell projecting the sell,
I'm doing so well, but my set-aside
lifelines are unrefined and unshaped, every
element of character unmade- I can't even
remember who I used to be, how I used to
talk, how I used to be before the
catastrophe, the breakdown, the take, and
take, and take, and the shakedown. I've
forgotten all my old poetry- the style I had
that made fans and made people glad to
be around me is replaced by the sad shell
of personal hell raging inside me- it's not a
chronic condition- it's an admission to
pain, long-suffering, vain, yes, these veins
bleed blue blood of disdain and shame,
and the agony that a man can be is made

manifest in me like destiny. When I smile, you're seeing scars- old trust and new hope, fresh faced and ready for anything no longer, but pretending to be something like a shadow of what I used to see in the mirror. I'm not just broken, I'm blown up, disintegrated, fated it seems for a long life of half-empty happy moments and instigated half relief. This isn't a smile, it's loneliness, this mask I built, I made my home in this casket, and I won't die here, but I'll lie here and wait for the ground to move and prove these moves, that it was all worth waiting in pain until I could finally smile again, because I'm a moth to a flame with a name but every word that breaks open my lips is pain.

It's just one of those days.

April 11, 2015

I know I promised you, dear, no more
poetry.

But damn if I can't help the way the scent
of you's still haunting me.

May 9, 2015

Honest as Air

*(Works best when read in an Irish accent, for
some reason)*

Lord, I do believe you made her for me.

She's no idol, no object of lust. But while

she's not here, she's a goal.

The future. The sunrise.

She's built perfectly, fit to me like joints,

bones knit together, and me to her.

Woven into my heart strings, this fabric,

this tapestry... I'd never hope to create

anything so lovely.

And when she cries. When her eyes are

weeping skies and clouded with storms

sending rivers down her face, my heart
reaches out through those strings and calls
out to hers in sorrow, in pain, in futile
desperate longing that I may be the
sunlight in her day, dry her eyes, kiss her
lids close, and call the summer sea to crash
kindly at her feet. Oh Lord, that she'd
know my heart!

I do believe it. Love. Why are we so
ashamed of the verb? Of the noun? Of the
name? I'm in it. I'm learning not to be
afraid of the implications. For the first
time in as long as I can remember, I'm
proud to say it. Oh love, I am in thee.
And when she laughs, like music does the
air around me sizzle and ring. It's electric,
and I am this simple, love-powered thing.
My engine creaks to life, and I roar like an
awoken lion. My function is to find her
scars and rub them with my fingertips

until they're gone. My highway is that which takes us to the stars, to pluck the perfect one like fruit from the vine of passion, that we may taste of its life-giving liquid until we close our eyes at last.

And I do believe she was built for me. Like the words you've given me, every melody and poetry. Like what you let me build for her, this chapel on a hill of green, this castle upon the world of words for all in love to find and see.

My dear, my love, her heart is broken and weak, beating frightened mewling whimpers there inside her chest. Aye, she's afraid of the great big world and it's cruel and pathological leaving. But she's braver than me. She's mighty in her dreams and in her mind are swirling brilliances awaiting their open door, when they may come rushing out upon the world and

paint it golden with her light. And I, my
soul, my heart is firm and strong, single-
set and sturdy, beaten down and burnt
with flame and all this wicked world may
throw. But for all that, I'm not that brave.
I'm not so sharp to pierce these iron walls
of reasoning away. I'm only clever with
some words I found, and most of them are
hers. But what I lack, you'll find in her,
and what I have will make her whole, and
though we're complete and perfect apart,
we've been designed to be a new machine
together. Like pieces to a simple puzzle,
whose only challenge is time and space.
Only dimensions could keep us apart. The
design is perfect, and the solution is
inevitable.

And should she chance to see this, perhaps
she'll smile. And when she does, I'll find
the brightest star, and know it's her heart

aglow, reflected in the sky.

For all the stars, maybe those heavenly lights, they're all little loves up there, just burning in the night.

For I do believe we were made for each other. And I am not ashamed. For we fit like fingers knit for only lovers then to name.

May 16, 2015

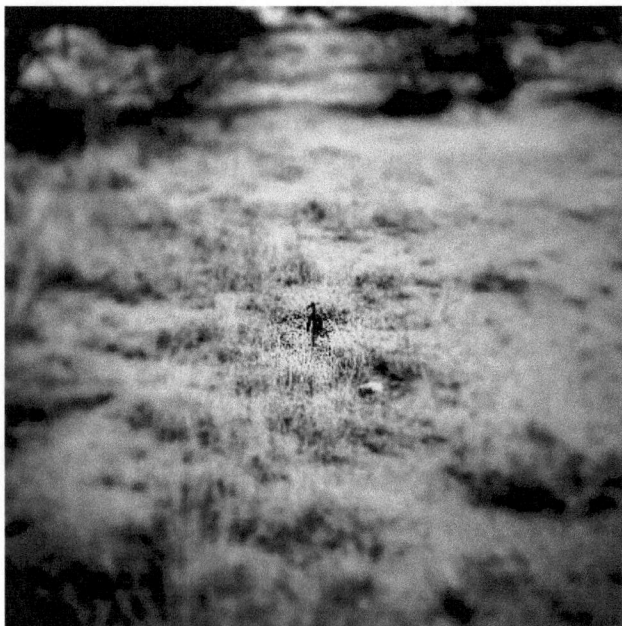

You are a rose-
Every petal is a fractured spiral
Leading to your fragile little
Lovely tender
Open heart.
Every simple bit of skin,
Every little curve,
You need not
Be so strong
Always.
Hide your thorns, little flow'r,
For you are delicate,
And in your delicacy
There is sweetness and
Perfection. There,
Little flower,
Bloom for me,
For life,
For you.

For all you are and will become.
You seedling.
Be so bold.
Hide your thorns.

May 22, 2015

How can someone like you
Own something so fragile?
So brittle with every word or touch,
And yet, dear, here, it's yours.

For someone so careless
And reckless with your touch,
This broken,
Beating thing is in your arms.

I've seen you shatter houses
And wiling to agree.
I've kissed you where it counts and
Sent you letters to believe.

So tell me now, my darling
How you do this simple thing-
How you take my heart in pieces
And refuse to fix the beats.

May 22, 2015

It's like a weight. Like a cloud, a fog, a shrinking, tightening mass that encompasses your entire body. It's like gravity pulling you everywhere, so no place feels secure. It's a desperate grasping at air, or trying to hold smoke. It's existential awareness of the possibility of utter impossibility. The belief that truly everyone is distant, that no one loves you, that you're on no one's mind, that you always make the first move. It's clawing for relevance against a diamondine wall. It's begging to be heard with a voiceless throat.

-an active analysis of depression

May 25, 2015

Falling in love is a series of severing heartstrings until the machine is suspended by only the one, and hung like an ornament of the soul behind your ribs.

If that last one is cut, you die. Your heart has to regrow its strings. You come back to life, like an old oak from winter. This is why people that have been hurt are so fragile. This is why they're so angry. This is why they're afraid. Someone swore they'd never let go, but they did. Their heart's been dropped. They're regrowing their strings.

It looks like loneliness, being in love, but it's not. It's prefect anchorage. A heart hung on one string becomes a pendulum, a metronome, a timepiece. It becomes more fully musical, rhythmic, and purposed. It meets its destiny.

Sometimes, we tear away strings with abandon. Sometimes strings we wish we'd kept become casualties. Sometimes, the strings seem too tough, so we subjugate them to blade, just in case they remain under normal methods, and remain unwanted. But that one... that single, prefect, diamondine filament... that one, we can never sever ourselves. That would be suicide from within. It can only be dropped.

Love with abandon. Find the thread.

May 26, 2015

I just discovered,
Oh my beloved,
That I can't write
More poetry.

For darling, all
That I may scrawl
Could never quite
Compare to thee.

May 29, 2015

A girl like that
Could shake the
world.
She'd quake your
bones
With just her
eyes.
A girl like I
Could never try,
She'd take the sea,
And paint your
skies.

You'd give her all
Your melody,

And feel just like
You've taken,
And leaving
wanting
More you wonder
How your soul's
So shaken.

A girl like that
Could trace the
stars
And wonders with
Her fingertips,
With every gentle
Brush of skin
And accident
Upon her lips.

A girl like that
Could be the
summer
Sky to a boy like
I can be,
And a girl like that
Could be the girl
Standing there
In front of me.

May 29, 2015

Oh, my precious little love,

Little flower in my eyes,

How you lighten, Precious Little,

Tender loving, careful comfort;

I would take your precious little

Heart in warming hands, in safety

And protect your precious little

Love forever, little beauty.

Precious little, little precious,

Precious little'd do you harm,

For my hands are strong and able

Just to hold you, Precious Little,

Safely from the night's cold gusts-

Piercing terrors in fright'ning shade-

Even though you, Precious Little,

Owe me nothing for this duty.

I do seek it, Precious Little,

Little starlight, little heaven,

Little angel on the ground,

I do keep it sacred, little

Picture of the most profound;

For I know that, Precious Little,

If your heart may gently rest,

Then I have done my work and earning.

Precious little love, my little light,

We are just little things

Here on this giant place we stand,

With little grass and little trees,

We are much smaller, Precious Little,

And our days are precious few,

But while you're holding, Precious Love,

My little heart, we're greater burning.

Precious little, Precious Little,

Love my precious life has seen,

And so my Precious Little Love,

So precious will yours ever mean.

Precious Little, darling light,
Precious grace upon your cheek,
Precious be the day and night,
Your precious smile I search and seek.

You're the same, in years and pain,
My Precious Little, just like me,
And in our eyes, like tears and rain,
Let, dear, precious love let free.

Oh Precious Little, mighty woman,
Brave and fragile, grown and strong,
Here's my precious little heart,
That you may keep it precious long.

May 29, 2015

Whatever you break,
Break it gently, my darling,
So I can fix it.

-ancient handyman proverb

May 30, 2015

To love, just throw your heart right at
A wall so hard it sticks.
At worst, at least you'll leave a mark,
That's really hard to fix.

May 31, 2015

Notes on Gravity

Pull this thing into the ground.
Bury it gently, with roses all around.
Soon the rain will go,
And the blossoms that we've sown will
bloom.

Take this thing into your heart.
Protect it now dear with your art.
Soon the day will fade,
And we'll wonder where our old loves
went to.

For all this gravity I still remain.
For all this turbulence, I'm still the same,
Just take my love, dear,
Take it where you rest your head.

For I'm yours, my darling, yours.
And I'll be here calling for you
And take these things
And keep them safe for you instead.

Nothing's quite so painful as no more.
I'd be lying if I swore I never dreamt of
you before,
So take this gravity
And let it at least lay you down.

Yes lover, you're just like the day I knew
you.
Lover, you're just like the day you knew
me too.
We're the sunset.
You're the sunrise, and I lay down.

For all this gravity,
I'd rather not escape.
But wait patiently
For you my wings
To make.

This isn't breaking.
It's building.
Endless building.
These castles are all yours.

June 3, 2015

In the interest of learning life lessons,
sequestered away from actionable modus:

Thou art she,
The desert rose,
The desert burn,
Lightening my eyes.

The stone broken,
Cut into my palm,
I bleed onto these
Mountainsides.

Thou art she,
The western wind,
The tempest
Raging against my skin.

The joy of wandering,
The love of longing,
The nearing horizon,
The rain. The rain.

Thou art she,
The moon and stars,

The holy handiwork,
Made evident.

The peace of pain,
The quiet flame,
The meadowlark,
The little bird.

Thou art she,
The far away,
The here inside,
The endless gasp.

The only loved,
The mystery,
The miracle of absence,
To me. To me.

June 13, 2015

Faces aren't so beautiful.
Even those familiar and lovely,
Don't hold their classic lustre.
Even a rose could never smell so sweet.
Darling, your eyes have captured,
The light of the stars.
Your smile shines brighter,
Than our lovely waning moon,
Whose delicate crescent
Is ever prefect to behold.
If I miss thee,
It's as missing gravity,
Where I live afloat,
Until my feet fall upon
Solid ground.
But when I see you,
I've landed,
And found my path
Back home.

June 16, 2015

Every second. Every breath. She steals my
heart. She makes it beat.

June 19, 2015

The Two Little Puppies

Once upon a time in a place not so far
There lived an old Mastiff by the name of
Lamar.
He lived all alone with one bowl and one
bone,
And he whimpered himself nightly to
sleep.

One day the old pooch was tied up to his
stoop,
Just looking out upon the neighborhood
loop.
There now before him, the two who'd
adore him,
The two little puppies, one big and one
small.

The big one was shy, but as clever as wind,
He had one crossed eye, and a hilarious
grin.
He'd hop all around, and he'd make silly
sounds,

And he ran up to Lamar and he gave him a
kiss.

The little one, he was as solid as rock,
And he'd grumble like thunder and fly like
a hawk.
So fast though he was, he was still made of
fuzz,
He came right up to the old dog and
nuzzled his chin.

The big puppy said "hey there, daddio!
"Where are you going, and why don't you
go?"
The old dog said "son, I'm afraid I've
forgotten,
"How to run, sitting here with my bowl
and my bone."

The little one cried and he pricked up his
ears!
With a scream he said "no!" and hunched
up on his rears.
With a powerful bound, he made right for
the rope,

And he bit it in two with his mightiest
bite.

Well, the old dog stood up, still then not
quite sure,
For his wobbly bones were uncertainly
cured,
But he trusted these pups, for they loved
him so true,
And he'd never known something like love
then so sweet.

He stood on the stoop and he made his
way down,
Slowly at first, but soon he did bound,
As the strength in his muscles and heart
did return,
And he followed those two little puppies
around.

As it turns out, those brave little pups,
Still needed Lamar to protect them from
stuff,
So he discovered his love and he new-
found his joy,

Just following those two little puppies
around.

One day, Lamar, the mighty old dog,
Was resting in shade of a toppled-down
log,
The puppies were playing, one big and one
small,
At his feet, they were practicing war.

He opened one eye to request they played
nicer,
But what did his eye then behold in the
light there?
The most beautiful creature that he'd ever
seen,
Smiling at him and his pups on the
ground.

She trotted on up to Lamar and said "hi."
Lamar was still stunned by the blue of her
eyes,
So he just wagged his tail and smiled his
widest,

And she sat beside him and his pups on
the ground.

Many years later, the puppies had grown.
They found themselves love and they
found themselves homes
But old Lamar was never any longer alone,
All thanks to those puppies, one big and
one small.

June 20, 2015

Sunset fires as cliffs cut the sky.

New Ways

You should be so many diamonds,
The starlight, the rain,
You should be the gentle breeze,
You should let me bear your pain.
You should have the sunlight,
And you should have the summer's kiss,
And you should have the winter white,
And you should be the autumn bliss.

So soft, my sweet, so lovely,
So gently breathe your words,
So passionate, beloved,
Let us make new language heard.
You should have the wonders,
The mountains and the seas,
Yours are opal sunsets,
And ceilings made of leaves.

You're a virtue, so sweetly said,
You, the whisper on my lips,
You, the blood in my veins sacred,
You the tune in my fingertips.
You should be, you tigress,
You should be, you dove,

And know all of the new ways
I can find to say I love.

Let it never age or die,
And let it never cease to mean,
And let us take out hearts and fly,
And let us conquer anything.
And let me tell you every word,
And let me fill your days,
With every little song I've heard,
And let us find new ways.

June 21, 2015

There are these days,
Like today, when fairly,
You can simply lift your eyes,
And taste the sky.

When silence is full,
Of these prefect little melodies,
These simple golden moments,
Those gently flying sparks.

Oh my darling,
This is the day, love,
Where everything's in color,
And we lose no light.

Where everything between us,
Is shared, given, taken,
Wasting nothing, wanting naught,
But melted together into stronger steel.

Oh my love,
This is the summer,
This is the dream,
This is the beautiful beginning.

June 25, 2015

There's magic in the music of the
movement of your voice,
Like challenges so chosen, ever charming
in your choice.
These, the thirsty thoughts that there my
thorough wonders think,
Where love your life is lived like lost old
legends at last linked.
And then, my darling daring desperately
deserving dear,
In nothing, neither wonder, nor
neglecting, never near,
Oh my love, oh darling wonder, lovely
marvel, little bird,
The music in your voice, the only song
I've ever heard.

July 1, 2015

I closed my eyes for a moment,
And found you smiling at me.
My heart leapt inside,
And my lungs filled with air,
And I realized then, love,
That even the thought of you,
Unprepared, and unexpected,
Unplanned, and unlooked for,
Is just as sweet and perfect
As the first time I saw you.
You've put a fire in me,
And even oxygen burns it brighter.

I've discovered the simple science of
breathing.

July 2, 2015

We were made for each other,
In the land before the stars,
Darling, our souls were knit together,
Our hearts made in corresponding tempos.

We were built from common clay,
And made into fitted shapes,
And even though time is long,
Our pieces still fit the same.

You were hewn from precious stone,
And I from something crude,
But you bind to me like a kiss,
And my breath is yours to take.

And 29 years, I've known you.
And 29 years, I've loved you.
And 29 years, I've missed you.
And 29 years you've gone.

And now, love, how you've grown,
And now, dear, how you've become,
And now perfected, love, as we can be,
How we've crossed this divide.

And 29 years, I've been walking,
And 29 years, I've looked,
And 29 years, dear, to find you.
How 29 years fly by.

And finally, it's finished.
And finally, I'm yours.
And at long last my arms can be filled,
The love they've hungered for.

July 3, 2015

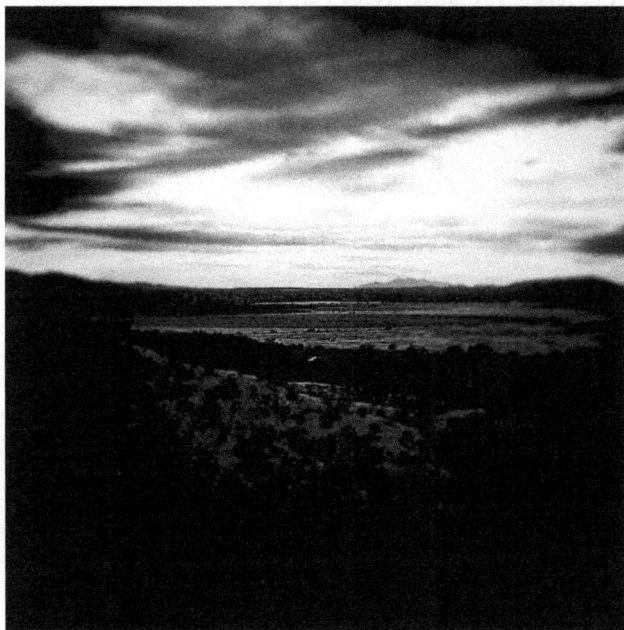

Maybe the sky pays blue homage to
your eyes.

Maybe the sunset is a pink and golden
promise.

Perhaps, my dove, every heart carved
Into every maple
Is a love note left by prefect strangers,
For you on my behalf.

What if the world conspires dearly
To love us here together,
And paint my days with amber hues,
And yours with little love songs?
Because it seems that way,
Every time I wake and listen to the breeze.

Maybe, love, life isn't perfect,
And I am certainly far from pure,
But amidst our subtle scars,
There live these little wonders,

Marvels beholden to every

Careful placements of our hearts.

Maybe the Earth shakes beneath the feet

of love.

Maybe the rain comes to cool the heat of

pain.

Maybe the summer sheds our skin,

Maybe it burns ourselves away,

And makes us, darling, simple,

Quiet beings of no pretense.

Maybe the day I saw you was the day I

awoke,

When ugly words found simpler meanings,

And music fell into place,

And planets decided to align in

celebration,

One more peaceful, simple, perfect,

Ever-living love. Can you feel it?

July 4, 2015

In golden dusk, with a million downy stars
Drifting gently lower through waning sunlight,
You were there, on my arm, singing our song.

As the daylight drew it close around us,
With a hundred little lovers passing by,
You were there, the word on my lips.

Children laughed and spoke their awe,
People held closer than in winter chill,
You were there, fire in my sky, the supernova.

Explosions of diamonds and gemstones,
My heart stopped beating in moments,
You were there, a sweet eternity of lovely instances.

If we're allowed but one perfect memory,
I'm blessed to find it so young, my love,
For you were there, when time stopped,

and we were living in the space between
seconds.

Halcyon Days.

So let me take the hours,
Let me color them and glaze,
And I'll make of them a perfect
Picturing of all the ways
You're the smile on my lips,
And even electricity,
For when it's you I kiss,
You're the last thing that I see
When I close my tired eyes,
And when you take my shaky hands,
You're the strength inside my bones,
And the ground on which I stand.

Oh, my little soul, push not so
Forever strong,
For she's the gentlest of angels,
She's the sweetest of songs.

July 5, 2015

Penguin Problems

The penguin looked into the sky
And said "Oh where, my love, is she?
For here I stand upon the ice
Betwixt the mountains and the sea."
And so he trod the tundra 'neath
His tough and webbed little feet,
In search of one who'd march along,
His happy heart in love to meet.

He walked amongst those fellow birds,
But not a one was he to find,
To place upon, his simple words,
Or give away his heart to bind.
"Alas!" he said, just then resigned,
To tread the glass at last alone,
For there was work to be refined,
In finding fish and making home.

And so the penguin grew his might,
Dove headlong into the sea,
And practiced hard all day and night,
To amplify his mastery.
For he was sleek and swift and strong,
And meat he could indeed provide,

And in the water was his song,
Where with flourish and fleet he'd glide.

One day while then courting life,
He happened to be making waves,
When suddenly he found his wife,
There swimming fast within the caves.
And Oh! She was of rarest beauty,
Black as stone and white as snow,
He looked at her and knew his duty,
To give to her there his heart to know.

He never swam so fast before,
Then as he called out after her,
"Beloved, meet me on the shore!
And I shall be thy passenger!"
She giggled in her penguin way
"You silly little penguin man,
I'll meet you there up in the day,
But you must first catch me if you can!"

There beneath the icy blue
She flew and spun in cursive flight,
And he made chase like lovers do,
And swore to never leave the fight.
They'd twist and twirl cunning lines,

Their dance a perfect symphony,
And then at last, their love defined,
She led him there out of the sea.

And on the icy beach they stood,
And found their love there in their eyes.
She said "you'll keep me safe and good?"
He said "I'll never tell you lies.
I'll make this frigid place your home,
I'll shelter you from gale winds,
And you shall never be alone,
And you will be to me my kin.

"I'll love you in the summer melt
And warm you in the winter storm,
I'll battle any threat you felt,
And ever keep you safe from seal harm.
I'll love you when you're off for food
And keep your egg off of the ground,
I'll build you up with magnitude,
And dance with you into the sound.

"And when you're feeling tired, love,
From all the work you have to do,
I'll kiss you sweet upon your beak,
And shout for joy and cheer for you."

She smiled and took his shaky wing,
And kissed him on his penguin cheek.
"Then this shall work," her voice did sing,
And then his penguin skin went pink.

They waddled back to all the rest,
Who shouted out with victory,
"Our penguin friend," they did digress,
"Has found his love there in the sea!"
The penguin dance they had that night
Was unlike any ever known,
For never was so sweet a sight,
As those two penguins coming home.

July 5, 2015

Oh sweet mercy,
Would that I were
Made of weaker stuff!
For I would bite
Back upon cruel fate,
With uncommon vengeance.

July 6, 2015

Something burns
In this new
distance,
Makes its turns
Against this
instance-
Maybe it's
The justice failing,
Perhaps it's
Just simple
flailing;
In the moment
I tried to hold
There on to smoke
And taste the
gold,
But only found
My left hand
empty,
And in my right,
My homework
kept, be-
-fore the
nightmare
Turned to stone;
The lovely life
there
Was my home,
And in the night,
While I was
sleeping,

Somewhere there
Was someone
weeping,
Wishing there
were
Some more stars
Upon her sky,
For even ours
Were falling, and
She missed the
lovely
Way they fell
Upon her only,
But the simple
Fact is that
She was
surrounded
Even fast,
And there in
darkness
There in life,
Music was stolen
From my life
By some low
creature
Lost in waiting-
Made to make her
Best for hating-
Take her virtue,
Turn it tender,
Let her lovely

Heart surrender
There upon
The ground to
losing
The one thing
Her heart be
choosing,
And instead
Confound her
mercy
With the tempest
Of her hurt, she
Held smoke too,
once
Never met,
But having held
Never forget.
So in this
wasteland
Of my heart,
All that I have
Is empty art,
For she is
somewhere
Shining like
The stars within
The summer
night,
And I keep falling
Into love,
With her, my

gentle
Little dove,
And wishing that
This time would
pace,
And let my broken
Turn to haste.
For nothing new
Within the day
Begins to cross
Upon dismay,
And heavenly
She is to me,
But far away
She must remain,
I guess, for I
Must now suppose
That heavens burn
When you get
close,
And I will stand
Upon the shore,
And thirst be first
And love before,
And mercif'ly
Protest in silence
For I love her
For I'd die. This
New defeat,
This crippling
blow,

This agony
Is mine to know,
So bleed the
wound,
And kill the song,
And make the
grave,
And make me
strong.
This is the game
You choose to
play,
And I will play it
Every day
To keep you from
Such dulling skies
That keep the
magic
From your eyes.
There was even
Magic there
Above your chin,
Beneath your hair,
And somewhere
we
Were lost in
fighting
For the day,
And for the night.
We lost it in
The gentle shove,
In which we,
starving,
Searched for love,
And found it, but
We grasped too
strong,
And killed the
fragile
Little song-
My love, we'll
make
New melodies,
And find more
perfect
Songs to sing.
And 'til then,
heart,
Strong patience of
And calling into
Skies above;
For thunder, stike
me
Down, I say,
For without her,
I waste away.

July 7, 2015

I admire your conflict.
The heart that burns
Within you, my dear,
Is perfect.

I envy not your pain,
But I do love it.
Your agony, my dear,
Is near to me.

Your passion is palpable,
A visible wave,
Even here, my love,
I feel your gravity.

Your sorrow is food to me,
I taste it bittersweet,
Unsavory candy,
Like biting down upon a stone.

Your heart is rare silver,
Your love, tempered gold,
Your beauty, a fracture across my sky,
A lightning strike.

July 7, 2015

God, grant me the strength to change
the things I cannot accept,
The serenity to accept the things I cannot
change,
And the wisdom to know the difference.

Give me the grace to know her heart,
To love her absence as the traveling dove,
To hold her silence, dear masterwork.

Allow me peace to gentle her visage,
To hold her eyes so sweet in mind,
And keep her safe in every thought.

To hold her dear in gentle hands,
And lest she break, every touch be sure,
And in every lovely loss be pure.

July 8, 2015

Slow burn,
Like a leaden
candle,
Let it rest.
And let it go.

Still turn,
Like a molten
metal,
Shape it lest
It never grow.

Make then,
As you ought to
music,
Let it foster,
Let it learn.

Take then,
As you need,
dear, use it.
Let it wander.
Let it groan.

We have
Made something
ugly.
We have

Made something
hurt.

Claim you
This perfect
glory-
Let it founder,
Let you yearn.

I make
None less than
stories.
I make
None less than
turns.

You are
the swiftest glory,
And the joy
I almost learned.

We are
The saddest story
That, my love,
I've ever heard.

You found
Your heart beside
you.

You said
Your heart beat
wrong.

I think
You found inside
you
You feared
Your heartbeat's
song.

Keep you
My love in
waiting.
Keep you
My love like far.

Let them
Be even always.
Let them
Be even ours.

For you made
The night shine
brighter.

You made
The twilight stars.

I am
The stone
unstop'ped
I am now
Composed of
scars.

Let me then, love,
Wait in silence.
Lay me then,
love,
Wait apart

Oh, my fear
Your breath
betrays you.
Little sweet,
Your breath does
harm.

July 9, 2015

I am unwell.
I find the day swelling,
Rolling like a bloody sea.

I find a tremor
In a moment of silence,
Quaking like a stricken tree.

I collapse,
Into dark blue mourning,
With shadows that fall like stones.

And scream aloud,
A hurricane through shuttered windows,
My voice is gone, alone.

Yes, I am unwell,
For I am somehow joyful,
And still I somehow breathe.

I find in this
Raging absence,
She still inspires the sick in me.

I am her walking casualty.

July 11, 2015

Fall into bed, it's been a long day.
I exercised some of my demons away.
Whisper goodnight to your ghost, and a prayer;
Sometimes I know you still hear me out there.
Close my wet eyes with a sigh and asleep,
And try to forget all the secrets I keep.

July 14, 2015

I want to sail you,
The sky of diamonds,
Swim in your eyes for a hundred years.
I want to bind,
To combine,
To make a memory of all your tears.
I want to sleep in your shadow,
And wake in your whisper,
Be so lovely.
Dove, how you've been,
Glory, now I breathe,
And you've made a minstrel of me.

July 20, 2015

The Lion and the Butterfly

The lion found himself
Within the favor of the butterfly,
And there he saw her perfectly
Within the wonder of his eye,
And somehow in her beauty,
She alighted there upon his paw
And danced for just a moment where
He held her still in all his awe.

He flicked his gaze up Heavenward
So grateful for his little gift,
And whispered secret gratitude
For even she his heart did lift,
And in his tangled mane between
Two lonely orbs between his ears
His incomprehensible love
Did then defect his ancient tears.

He held her soft upon his claw
And cradled her with all his might,
And dreamed that she might dream with
him,
And share her beauty in the night.
He rested soft upon the glade

In amber light within the set
Of sun upon his golden flax,
And never her splendor forget.

And in the morning, when he rose
He searched for her in all the world
But find her not, he did indeed,
And lose her fast, his love unfurled.
And so he looked, and so he sought,
And so he pondered in his ploy,
And in all this, he found her nought,
But crushed her there in all his joy.

For so he found her in the dirt,
All mangled, broken, crippled, crushed,
For while he dreamed, he loved her so,
And pressed her bones into the dust,
And as he held her body loft,
He bellowed to the God above
That mercy strike him down at last
And kill him with his final love.

But soft, the breeze did prick his flesh,
And draw the marrow from his bones,
For there was nothing left to death,
But just his empty lion clothes.

He cried into the night and day,
And begged the life to fast return
But lion cries are never loved,
And lion pleas are never heard.

And thus the lion set his skin
Within which his heart once dwelt
Unto the task of living in
The beauty that his life once felt,
And sealed the harangue of his chest
Behind steel walls even of pride,
And swore to life never forget
The favor of the butterfly.

July 23, 2015

The Tangible Benefits of Dying Alone

I may never die alone-
I may die in house and home
Alongside someone I love
And say their name goodbye.

I may never sing to sleep,
So gently into tragedy.
I may just rest in sweet repose,
And lie there, die alone.

I may not ever hear the cry
Of someone bidding me goodbye.
I may not ever hear the weep
Of someone scared to sleep.

I could just pass into the night
With poetry by candlelight,
And my last words will ever be
Thank you for not think'ng of me.

The truth is that no matter what
My final moments hold, and but
The tragedies that lie in me
Are mine alone to keep.

So maybe I'll not die alone,
And maybe I'll not have a home,
And perhaps I'll just buy the stars
And keep them then with me.

For somewhere, love, in all the night
And somewhere there with all your might
You trumpet all your appetite
And leave me here alone.

But here I am in solitude,
And yes my love, I think of you,
But even if I die today
I die at least alone.

July 24, 2015

Maybe you can fly.
Maybe you have all your feathers,
Lovely little soul.
How I love to watch you soar.

I imagine we were made,
Maybe we were made for us.
I keep expecting you
To walk through every door.

Day and night, I look.
I gaze upon horizons and see you,
Stabbing the sky,
With all your perfect lines.

I see you far and near.
I see you in memories I've yet to build.
I know you now,
I know you then, refined.

I find you in sleep,
My whiskey cries.
There's a wonder here,
In this castle's future stones.

Maybe you can fly,
But so can I, darling.
I'll race you to the stars and back,
Aloft and not alone.

July 28, 2015

Hapy

How many four letter words
Do you know?
How many times do you love
And let go?
How many dreams that may be dreamed
Have you dreamed
When the curtain draws at last
To its close?

Where are the moments
You'd sworn never leave?
Where are the mysteries you'd
Never dare believe?
What if I could tell you that
It's all contained in space
Out of time, out of room
Out of place?

Sometimes there it lies
In a lover's tender kiss.
Sometimes it resides
In a still surrendered bliss.
Sometimes it's the tears in eyes,
And sometimes words on lips.
Sometimes it may even rest
On toes or fingertips.

Often, I have found,
It's the spaces between words,
In the silence, in the distance,
In the meaning, in the verbs.
It's the moments between waking
And the moment sound asleep,
And the stillness within quaking
And her heart between its beats.

Where can you find perfect,
My beloved, little joy?
It's the masterpiece in breathing,
It's the wonderment deployed.
Where do you build trust upon-
An island or a range?
Is it founded just of virtue,
Is it pressed into a page?

It is lovely, dear I say to you,
It's air, it's sun, it's rain, it's sky,
It's patiently awaiting days,
That never may they pass us by.
It is braving all the tempest and
The whirlwinds that can be.
It's the sweet, the smile, the laugh,
The heart, the eyes that make us hapy.

July 30, 2015

The mark of one given up on life is a certain vacant pleasantness. This is me smiling. Heaven take me.

August 3, 2015

Hell hath no fury, indeed. I just want to give her a hug. Ow, my heart.

August 5, 2015

Maybe the worst part of a broken heart is knowing it'll heal. Perhaps we mourn the impermanence of it. That, no matter how much you love(d) someone, even they couldn't destroy you. Maybe secretly we all, if we can't keep a hold on something that fills our hearts with sincere and innocent joy, would rather it destroyed us. For if something you loved couldn't also kill you, there's a palpable disappointment at the unworthiness of the object.

August 7, 2015

The Beautiful Broken

Do you see her there, who once sewed
flowers through her hair, but now where
only raven plumage grace her heavy
fractured crown? Whose lovely withered
little soul has weary waned to empty hole,
and eyes have dimmed their light inside
her brow? Take her poisoned blood that
runs like ink inside her veins, and let her
beautifully broken to the ground.

August 16, 2015

The Gentleman, The Devil

The apple once was plucked, his long and
slender fingers skillful pulled, and handed
he it to the woman clothed in heaven's
light.

He said "my darling little bird, why do you
there so sweetly long so sadly for the just
remains of quite so little appetite?

"For in your eyes, as blue as seas, I find
myself reflected there, so lovely now you
look to me as though you were in stars
tonight."

She smiled then gently through her woes
as upon this kind stranger met, her eyes in
his unwaver'd gaze so sharp unto her
sweet delight

And took from him his apple drawn down
from in the tree of misery, where once was
told into her heart that never she should
taste its bite.

"But worry not, my dear, my love, for
never you shall know the pain of what you
fear for in this pomme are mysteries
beyond your sight,

"And in this heart, when once the flesh is
pierced within your cunning lips, your love
shall come and savor too and savor you
with all his might,

"But be it not beneath my will to tell you
now how sweet you are, that I may have
you now my dear, and take your love with
me this night,

"For thou art golden treasure fair, and I
should keep thee well and strong, if you'd
but take this gift from me and let me fill
your soul with fight."

And so she took from him the apple of his
eye and knew its taste, and fainted fast for
him, in love, and took his hand, he took
her tight,

And took her home, the devil did, the
gentleman, the serpent there, and led her
through the corridors of verdant wood and
holy white.

He led her by her eager hand, imprisoned
soul, up to the peak, where she beheld the
earth below and there believed in all her
right,

Where she there stood entrapped in love
for this fair man so shrewdly gained, and
fast he kept her shackled there believing
she had seen the light.

August 18, 2015

My love. My love is everyone. My love is the strange and the unfamiliar. My love is the foreign and the unassigned. My love is the distant and the incoherent. My love is the quiet and afraid. My love is the silence, and my love is the noise. My love is the inconvenient, the accidental, the bemused, and the unexpected. My love is the alive and the unprepared. My love is in every moment, and every breath. My love is perfect, unafraid, and unbidden. I love, recklessly, with abandon.

August 24, 2015

I couldn't be happier. The people I love the most are right here with me. This is why I'm here.

August 25, 2015

Tears of light that grace the night and find the fight in all of us. So then we find, to our delight, the presence of the call of us.

August 25, 2015

In twenty four hours, I'll be statuesque,
Trying my very best to blend into a wall,
Wishing with all I have for you to see me.
And in that moment, the one where you
do,
When our eyes cross like stars shot at
moons,
Will a smile bloom across your lips like a
rose?
Will your small pools fill with their liquid
love?
Will I remain, or will your gravity break
me up,
Away from my safe perimeter, from walls,
Unto you, hurtled through nothing lightly,
Like meteors crashing into your space,
Innocently falling through your clear,
Sacred atmosphere, to burn up?
Or will I remain, apart, longing for it?

But the look, I do not require, nor the
smile,

No, not even for the touch of embrace do
I pine.

It is simply the beat of your heart nearby.

Almost audible, the way it falls,

Always clear to me,

Matching mine.

Love,

Me.

August 29, 2015

I'll stand here with this mountain on my shoulders.

I don't mind. I really don't. I am much stronger than you think.

I'll walk your poison road beneath each of these foul boulders.

Even if into the fallow ground I always ever sink.

I'll carry this into my ancient grave.

I've set my jaw, my teeth ground into dust in misery.

But I don't care. I truly don't. You weren't up to me to save.

I've steeled myself against you long before I was a memory.

Oh, sweet, deadly, toxin. I remember you, dear jade.

I've never seen someone so ugly, and so sweet.

How dare you exist the way you do, oh symphony?

I found you in the stars one day...

Remember me?

I was the smile you scraped off of your face, so eagerly.

I didn't hear you laugh one time. Not once. You sold your soul to the devil for some peace.

Well, I'm a hurricane. Remember me.

August 31, 2015